OLD TIME
WHITTLING

Easy Techniques for Carving Classic Projects

Keith Randich

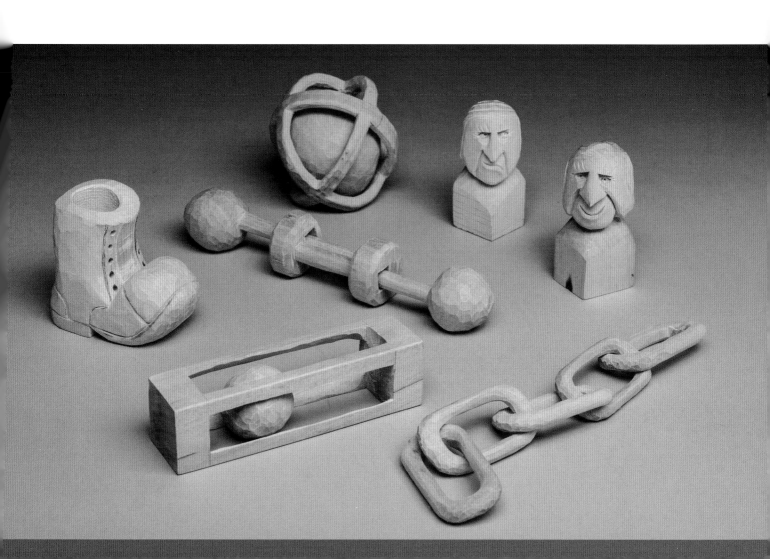

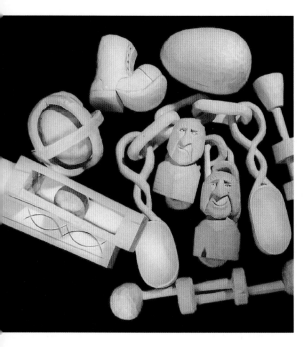

ISBN 978-1-56523-774-2

To learn more about the other great books from Fox Chapel Publishing, or to find a retailer near you, call toll-free 800-457-9112 or visit us at *www.FoxChapelPublishing.com*.

Note to Authors: We are always looking for talented authors to write new books. Please send a brief letter describing your idea to Acquisition Editor, 1970 Broad Street, East Petersburg, PA 17520.

Printed in China
First printing

Table of Contents

• •

Introduction

There used to be a time when people had the knowledge and skill to take materials they had at hand and create things they needed to survive. One such material was wood, as trees stood in abundance. Although the objects people created were not permanent, the wood was able to be worked by the few tools they possessed. Once their shelter was complete and the livestock penned, they built articles that added to their comfort. As their lives improved and time permitted, they would use their woodworking skills to produce items for ornamentation and entertainment. A chair, a spoon, and a bowl were designed to fill utilitarian purposes, yet each one became an object of decoration in the hands of a whittler during the long, cold winters. Toys were created for children, chests for blankets, and boxes for pipes, tobacco, and other items of value.

Eventually, towns appeared and businesses were able to provide many of the items that people had once been forced to create for themselves. Laws of fashion and social status dictated that homes be equipped with items produced of shiny materials from faraway places. As the necessity to create faded, so did the knowledge and skills that so many once possessed. For many years, only a small number of artisans, and a smaller number of hobbyists, carved furniture for well-to-do individuals and other objects for the secular trade.

I find it interesting that the last thirty years have seen a rebirth of handcrafts such as woodworking and woodcarving. In the same period of time that we have seen so much technology put in place to enable us to do less and less work, thousands of folks are going back to activities that our ancestors did out of necessity. It's as if a large segment of the population gave up their TV remotes, multi-channel cable, and leather recliners and decided that performing might be a little more interesting than being a fulltime audience. After a day on the rock pile, they found a couple of hours spent in front of the workbench a much more creative release than taking in the network's new fall lineup.

The term "whittling" conjures images of old men making shavings while sitting on a bench in front of the general store. My definition of whittling (and Webster backs me up on this) is simply any carving done with a knife. Carving implies the use of chisels, gouges, and a mallet, while sculpting is just carving while wearing a beret with a plump nude sprawled out in front of you. Feel free to substitute any of the three terms when speaking to your friends and family.

Copyright H.T. Webster
NY Herald Tribune Syndicate

The intent of this text is to distribute some of the lost knowledge of whittling back to people who are tiring of playing the spectator role and are looking for an avenue to channel their creativity.

The text is ordered in such a way that skills taught in one project are built upon in the next. This book differs from many other instructional carving books in that I really try to present each step separately. It means we'll start out slowly, but I guarantee you'll know which end of the knife to push by the time you've completed a couple of projects.

Pictured are pine (top left and bottom right), basswood (light wood on left), and tupelo (middle).

Wood

• •

Basswood (linden) is the most popular wood for whittling in this part of the world. It is soft enough to allow working with hand tools, yet its close grain allows it to hold fairly good detail in a carving. It is readily available in varying thicknesses at lumberyards and craft stores and remains relatively inexpensive.

Whittling draws an image of taking a knife to whatever wood one has at hand, and any soft, straight-grained timber will do nicely. Butternut, chestnut, redwood, yellow poplar, tupelo, cottonwood, some pine, and cedars all carve well. Stay away from balsa wood—it's just too soft. Oak and walnut are great carving woods, but you'll have a tough time carving them without a mallet and chisel. Don't be afraid to experiment. There is a great variety of possible woods; feel free to try woods not listed in this book. Many local woods are great for carving, but because of their limited range and lack of commercial availability, often don't show up on the list of carving woods. I've received samples of obscure species sent by students and readers living in areas that produce trees that are considered exotics in the Northeast part of the country.

Because we're using our bare hands to pull a knife through wood, avoid wood with knots in it or pieces with obvious twists in the grain.

If you are fortunate enough to find a local tree service or your neighbor is cutting down a linden or cedar, rush to the scene with baubles for bartering. Even a healthy pruning of a mature tree can put you in fat city in terms of your wood supply. Be sure to split the logs from the tree to speed the drying process. Store your cache out of the sun but away from any heat source. Drying a log too quickly will promote checking and cracking. The rule of thumb for air-drying wood is a year per inch of thickness, although softer woods will dry sooner. You'll need to bring the wood inside for a few months before actually using it. Watch the end grain carefully. If checks appear after the wood has been inside a couple of days, you probably brought it in too soon. Air-drying lumber is a hit or miss proposition, with most of the misses caused by impatience. Fortunately, the bad stuff can become practice stock or at worst, firewood.

I don't specify the size of the blocks I'm working with in some of the projects in this text. There is a tradeoff between using a big block that is easy to handle but takes longer to carve, and a small block that is difficult to handle yet carves quickly. I'll try to give a couple of dimensions that will work well. Otherwise, use the wood you have on hand and in the dimensions that feel most comfortable to you.

Knives and Keeping Them Sharp

The traditional whittler's tool of choice is his trusty pocketknife. Far be it for me to stomp on tradition this early in the text, but you are going to be hard-pressed to find a pocketknife these days that you can do much more with than put a point on a stick. Our pocketknives have evolved into folding utility knives. I guess the Boy Scouts, hunters, and the Swiss Army just aren't creating in wood like they used to. I'm suggesting that you acquire a simple carving knife to use with this book. You'll want a straight blade with a pointed tip, anywhere from 1" to 2" (25 to 51mm) in length. These knives are available at most woodworking, hobby, art supply, and craft stores, as well as mail-order supply houses.

You may find two distinct styles of carving knives, particularly at more well-equipped stores: fixed-blade knives, or knife handles with replaceable blades. Fixed-blade knives are less expensive and will work fine for our projects. The replaceable blade sets also work well, as the blades come very sharp. If you nick a blade edge, or simply can't get it as sharp as you'd like, simply pop in another blade.

Tool buying is a disease, albeit a survivable one. I have knives for every task and for each day of the week. Although I'd hate to deprive anyone from suffering through the symptoms of this affliction, I do want to point out that every project in this text can be accomplished with a single knife. But just in case—get well soon.

Sharpening rivals tools as the topic in most "my way is better" conversations among woodcarvers. For sharpening supplies, you can pick from stones, belts, or strops. If you select stones, do you go with oil, ceramic, water, or diamond? Is the stone spinning or lying stationary on a bench? How fast should the belt be moving? What grit of abrasive should you use? How about the strops—mounted on a board or attached to a hook like the barbers used to do? Power strop? What do you put on the leather— aluminum oxide, jeweler's rouge, WD-40?

Sound confusing? Why shouldn't it be? After all, a recent catalog from a woodworking supply house had more than nine pages dedicated to sharpening supplies. Every carver has his own favorite, and everyone's favorite is the best.

Let's get a couple of things straight. Number one, the biggest secret of successful carving (and in turn the biggest stumbling block for new carvers) is using sharp tools—very sharp tools. Forget about scratching thumbnails, cutting paper, or shaving arm hairs. A sharp knife needs to cut the fibers of the wood cleanly. Take a slice across the grain of a scrap piece of wood, and look closely at surface left by the cut. A sharp knife will leave a glass-smooth surface. On woods such as walnut and butternut, you'll actually see the pores in the end-grain of the wood. A less than sharp blade tears at the wood, leaves scratches, and requires more effort to push through the piece.

Second, sharpening encompasses two distinct steps: sharpening and honing. Sharpening is taking a tool and putting the correct bevel on its business end to allow cutting. Honing is taking that sharpened tool, removing any microscopic burrs left on the blade's edge after sharpening, and polishing the blade to create a fine edge. Many tools only require sharpening. Saw blades, axes, and many turning tools can go right from the grinder to the wood. Carving tools, carpenter's chisels, and knives need to have their edges further refined so they can be pulled or pushed through the wood with a minimum amount of effort.

Accomplishing these two steps requires different types of equipment. Grinding wheels, belts, and any stone described as "fast cutting" or "coarse" are used for sharpening. Leather strops and ceramic, polishing, or extra-hard stones are used for honing. A new knife purchased for whittling shouldn't need to be sharpened, but you will want to hone it until you're satisfied that it's really sharp. Once a knife is sharp, you shouldn't have to do anything more than hone it every now and then to keep it sharp, unless you nick an edge. I'll spend a minute or two honing my knives before and after my carving sessions and anytime I'm about to make a cut that I really need to cut cleanly.

And third, you should stick with any sharpening equipment and technique that you find comfortable. I've had an opportunity to try most of the offerings on the market at one time or another, and I assure you that they will all perform as advertised. Chances are that you'll try a couple different sharpening methods in your quest for the perfect edge. In this text, I'm going to use a strop charged with a honing compound, simply because it's probably the least

expensive method of honing. Strops are available from woodworking and woodcarving supply houses or can be made from a piece of belt leather about 18" (457mm) long and 1½" to 2" (38 to 51mm) wide (face it, it's been out of style for a few years now) glued to the edge of a board equal in width and a little longer to allow for a finger hold. A small amount of very fine abrasive material needs to be

applied to the leather, such as a polishing compound or one of the commercially available honing compounds. Now your strop is ready for action.

To hone your blade, place it at the end of the strop with the cutting edge trailing. Raise the flat edge slightly (about the thickness of a dime) and pull the knife the length of the strop. Flip it over and return the stroke. Don't push down too hard. It's important to remember to take long strokes while keeping the blade at a consistent angle.

Don't worry about honing a blade too much. Hone while planning your next cut. Hone when you find yourself having to push or pull just a little too hard. Hone when things aren't coming out right and you need a moment to think.

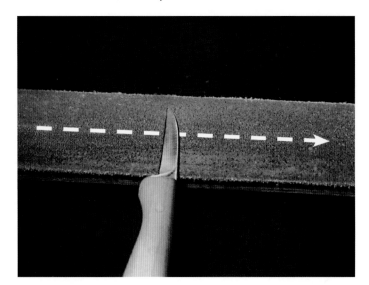

Safety

Before we jump into the actual carving, I want to make you aware of safety concerns relative to whittling. You're going to be pushing and pulling a razor-sharp blade into your thumb and within millimeters of your hands, so the potential for cutting yourself is quite real.

There are three things you can do to help combat accidents. One, keep your knife as sharp as you can. Most accidents occur when trying to force a dull blade through a cut. Rather than shearing the fibers, the blade gets caught momentarily and then fires through the wood due to the pressure exerted by the carver. If your knife doesn't glide through the wood, leaving a clean surface, spend some time at the strop before continuing carving.

Second, take controlled cuts. The knife should be placed in your hand right where your fingers meet your palm, with the sharp edge facing your thumb. Look at your hands relative to the blade's path before making each new cut. Start the knife slowly into the wood. If the blade gets caught, ease up on the pressure before the excitement starts. Remember, you're pushing a knife, not a wedge—more pressure won't help.

Third, wear a thumb guard on your knife hand. I realize the old-time whittlers didn't use them, but this is a new millennium, and we have to practice safe carving. God knows what back alley those knives hung around in before being sold to good homes like ours.

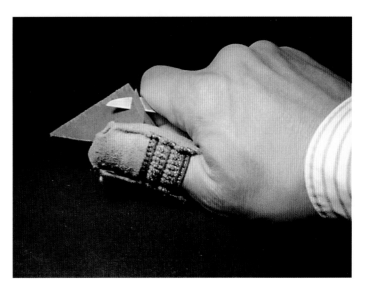

When making slicing cuts, you'll pull the blade through the wood in the direction of your thumb. As the blade exits the wood, it will bump into the thumb guard. It may not make sense to purposely pull a blade at your person, but it allows you to get power into the cut while still keeping control over the travel of the blade. Look for these guards in your local fabric stores, where they're sold for needlepoint, or your local woodworking supplier.

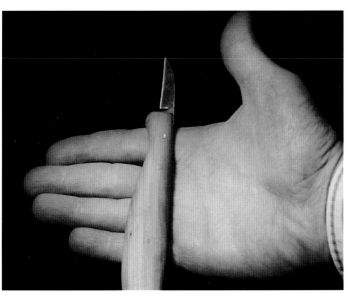

An Egg?

• •

An egg may sound like a pretty boring first project, but it is actually a great icebreaker for folks new to carving. It helps illustrate the laws of grain direction, and allows the carver to make slicing cuts both with the grain and across the grain. Although it's a very attainable object to create, it also helps to build strength in your hands (strength you didn't know you had).

Lay out your egg so the grain is running the length of the wood block. An egg is not a perfect spiral, so we'll carve ours off-center. Using a pencil, divide the egg into thirds on all four sides. Pick one end as the fat end, and connect your marks on that side with a heavy pencil line. This line is your starting point and will remain the fattest part of your carving.

The first order of business is to slice off the corners of the egg. Start your cuts at the pencil line, and pull your knife out to the end of the block. Keep turning the block as you go and knock off the highest remaining corners. Once this end of the block begins to appear round, rotate your block end-for-end, and again, starting at the pencil line, slice off the corners at the other end. Your block should resemble a cylinder at this point. Carefully

round the fat section, and draw your line back on. Your next step is to round over the ends. Up to this point, we've been making slicing cuts that have been parallel to the grain of the wood. Our next cuts will be at an angle to the grain. As you pull your blade through the wood at an angle, the fibers of the wood are sliced (if your knife is sharp), leaving two distinct surfaces on either side of the cut. One surface is left solid and straight (cut made with the grain), while the other has peeled back and split away from the blade (cut made against the grain).

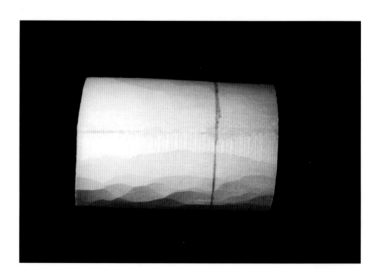

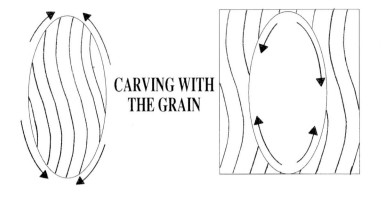

CARVING WITH THE GRAIN

The clean surface is what we want remaining on our egg, while the peeled back chip falls to the floor. Just to experiment, take tiny slicing cuts at the end of your block from a variety of directions. Cuts made with the grain will peel away, while those made against the grain will split. Whenever making a slicing cut, start it slowly. If it starts to split rather than slice the wood, change the direction of your cut.

Continue rounding each end. Pause occasionally, holding your egg at arm's length to inspect your progress. The closer you get to completing your carving, the finer your cuts will become. As you near the very tip, or axis, of the egg, your cut will be close to a 90° angle to the grain. You'll need to take a delicate cut with a sharp edge to leave a clean surface. Take a moment to hone the knife's edge before making this cut.

When your egg nears completion, take the time go over the entire piece and clean up your cuts. When creating a carving (or anything that requires a period of time to be dedicated) there is the temptation to hold up the piece and call it finished. I've made a habit of putting a carving aside for a couple of days before the final finishing. Then I'll spend a few minutes giving the piece the once-over with a knife that I use specifically for cleaning up my carvings. Carefully carve away any torn grain, pencil marks, fingerprints, and knife marks. Sanding your egg isn't cheating, but it doesn't make sense to spend all that time making clean cuts with a sharp knife just to sand all evidence of your handwork away.

You'll want to handle your egg often after carving it, so it will need a little protection. Oil or a spray sealer will seal the wood, and a coat of wax after a few days will give a soft glow to your creation.

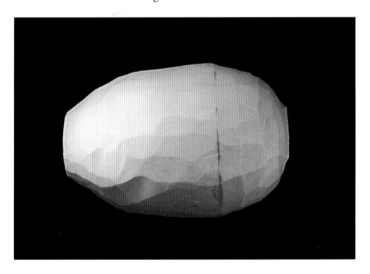

The Brogan

· ·

Our next project will be an old boot, also known as a brogan. I'll be using a 1½" (38mm) block for my brogan. This piece can be carved as a solid block, or if you want to use it as a toothpick or paperclip holder, you can hollow it out.

If you want your brogan hollowed, drill the block as your first step in order to take advantage of the strength of the entire block.

Draw the side view of the boot on your block so that the grain runs from toe to heel. Then, drill a ¾" (19mm) hole. If the hole didn't end up exactly where you wanted it, shift the layout of the boot to line up with it.

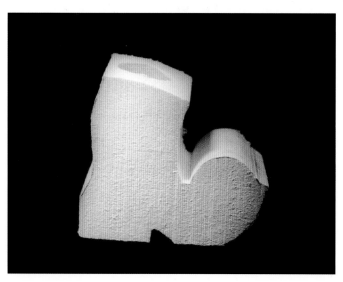

Rough out the profile of the boot. You can use a band saw, coping saw, or your knife.

Next, round off the toe of the boot. Keep in mind that a brogan has a big, bulbous area at the toe, so don't get too carried away when rounding. Remember the end of the egg—this will be the fat end.

Slice away from the sides, leaving the toe as the widest part of the boot. Keep the two sides balanced by looking at the underside.

Round the block from the heel up to the top. Begin your cuts on the sides, and slice forward to the tongue and back to rear of the boot. Check your progress by looking down on the boot.

Take a moment to refine your brogan. All cuts should be cleaned up. Any marks left by sawing need to be whittled away. Before starting to add any detail, we'll want to be sure that we've got the overall shape in balance. Look at your boot from a variety of angles to be sure that it appears to be an exact silhouette of a brogan. A mistake that many carvers make is to rush past the basic shaping of a project and begin to add the details. The consequences of not doing this step to completion are square heads, pear-shaped eggs, and in our case, boots that look like they still have the boxes on them!

On the sides and underside, draw a tiny vertical line to represent the front of the heel. Slice the wood away from the bottom in front of this line to a depth of ⅜" (10mm). The slice should taper from the ball of the foot back to the heel to give the boot its "lift." Draw a line around the block to represent the top of the heel and the sole, and make a stop cut on your line. Make a shallow slicing cut into that stop cut from above that line all the way around.

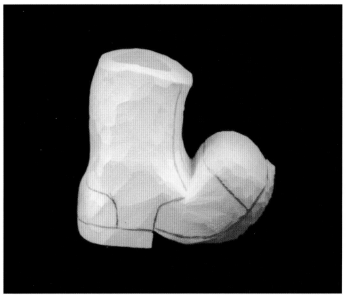

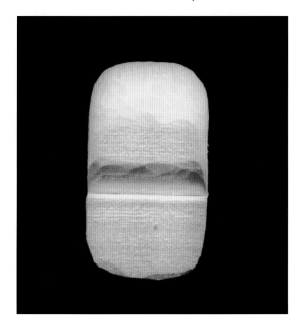

Draw a couple of vertical lines beginning at the base of the ankle to separate the tongue from the sides. Make a stop cut on these lines, and slice the wood away from inside them to give the tongue the appearance of being below the sides. Mark four or five eyelets on each side of the stop cut, and, using a tiny bit or the tip of your blade, bore in the holes.

For those that elected to hollow their boot, you can drill your eyelets all the way into the hollow.

Like most leather goods, a brogan is assembled by sewing a number of overlapping pieces together. We'll draw lines to represent the different pieces, and make stop cuts on the lines. The next step will be to make shallow slicing cuts on one side of each line to make it appear that one piece is overlapping another.

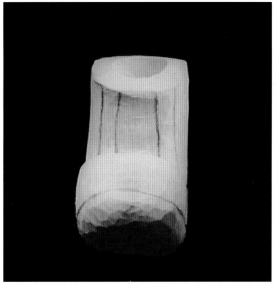

Make a second stop cut along the side of the first. This second stop cut represents the thread line holding the two pieces of leather.

Before applying any finish, take time to go over your piece and clean up your cuts. Be sure the stop cuts don't have any fuzz at the bottom. Any finish you apply will highlight all your mistakes, so don't rush past your last chance to do a good job.

To finish, apply a sealer first. Clear oil or spray acrylics will seal things nicely. Give it time to dry, and then put on a final coat of wax. Because this is a boot, you can use a wax-based shoe polish. Give it time to dry, and buff with a shoe brush, followed by a soft, lint-free rag.

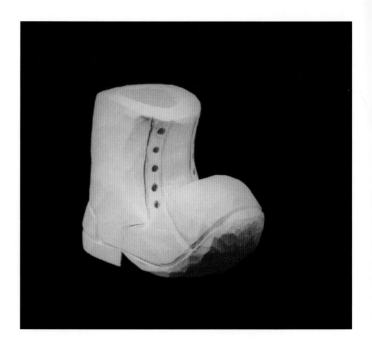

Ball-in-the-Cage

• •

A famous whittler's trick that has been around for a long, long time is the ball-in-the-cage. This piece requires you to take smaller and more delicate cuts as the carving progresses. Carvers in a hurry will inevitably end up with the equally famous, but not so popular whittler's trick called the ball-out-of-the-cage, or the-ball-and-the-pieces-of-cage.

Start with a block about 1" (25mm) square and 4" (102mm) long with the grain running the length of the cage. Draw a window around the cage on all four sides. The window is ½" (13mm) from the ends, and ¼" (6mm) from the long edges of the block. You should have a window measuring ½" by 3" (13 by 76mm) on each side. Split each window into three panes.

The center pane contains our ball. Our first task will be to do away with the wood in the two outside panes. You can use a ⅜" (10mm) bit and drill a couple of holes into each of the outside panes to help speed things along, or just whittle them away with your knife. Be very careful to stay inside your window lines.

The outside edges of the cage will be the bars of your cage, and if they become too thin, your ball will simply roll out.

Finish removing the wood from the outer sections. Make your stop cuts just inside the lines drawn, being sure to hold the knife perpendicular to the block.

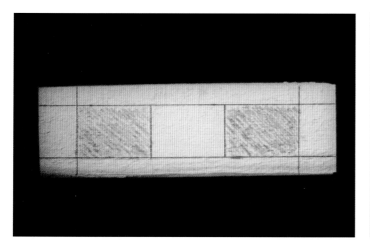

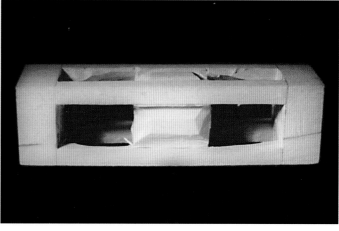

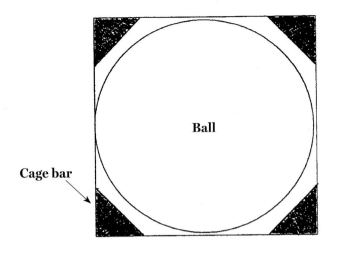

Ball

Cage bar

Start rounding the ball on all six sides by making stop cuts ⅛" (3mm) deep, and then making tiny slicing cuts inside the lines to pop out the chips.

The bars of this cage currently have four sides. In order to free our ball, we need to carefully shave away the inside of the bars to make them three-sided. This will enable us to reach inside to continue rounding the ball and eventually free it.

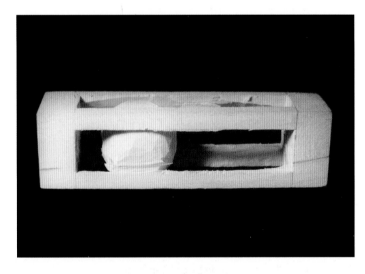

Once the ball is free, you will find yourself presented with a basic good news/bad news situation. The good news is the ball is free and still caged. The bad news is the ball is not completely round and it's very difficult to grasp through the bars. I've found that it helps to pin the ball in the corners of the cage to hold it. Take only tiny cuts to complete rounding the ball. Big slashing cuts have a tendency to break through the bars with alarming regularity.

Once the ball is round, you may move on to finishing the cage. I'm not a proponent of sanding any carvings, but we want to smooth the cage while removing the bare minimum of wood. If you do sand, however, keep one thing in mind: Don't use your knife on a surface once it has been sanded. Grit from the paper will be imbedded in the wood and will quickly dull your blade as you cut into it. Therefore, do any major cleanup with your knife first. Place a sheet of fine-grit sandpaper on a flat surface and sand the outside and ends of the cage clean. Lightly touch up the bars, but don't sand the ball. You'll want people to know you carved it.

Ball-in-the-cage carvings get handled quite a bit, so we'll need to put some type of sealer on ours. Dipping the piece in an oil finish or spraying it with a quick-dry acrylic sealer will work great. Try to avoid a heavy-coated or sticky finish. We don't want to gum up the works now.

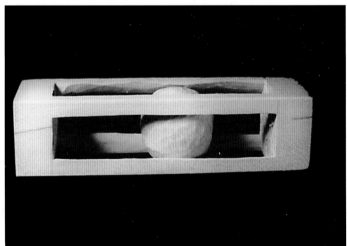

The Wooden Chain

• •

Another whittler's trick that has been around for a long time is the wooden chain. Wooden chains have been created that are hundreds of feet long. I have seen telephone poles chain-sawn into chains and tooth picks surgically incised into chains.

Start with a block about 1" (25mm) square and 6" to 8" (152 to 203mm) in length. With a pencil, divide the block into 1" (25mm) squares on all four sides. Draw 2" (51mm) links on each side of the block with interlocking links on the top and bottom. Note that the ends only have a half-link. Next, draw a couple of parallel lines the length of each side, ¼" (6mm) from the edge.

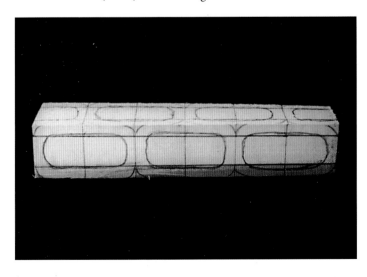

Slice away the corners of the block, being careful not to carve into the parallel lines. Make a stop cut into each of these lines and slice the wood on the outside of the cut. Continue making the stop cuts until you are ¼" (6mm) deep. At this point the side view of the block should appear as a long plus sign (+). (I prepare a couple dozen of these blocks for my classes, and in an effort to save time, the students start with a block in the "+" shape. Rather than carving my fingers to the bone, I set up my table saw to cut a ¼" x ¼" (6mm x 6mm) dado on each corner. If you think I may be bending the unwritten rules of whittling, consider the guy with the telephone pole and chainsaw.)

Draw your links back on the block. Take the time to draw both the inner and outer loop for each link. Make a shallow stop cut between the first two links. Widen that cut slightly by angling your blade to either side of that first cut. Continue until you have reached the bisecting link. Be careful not to cut through the bisecting link. Make the same stop cut between these links from the other side of the block.

Give your block a quarter-turn and make the same stop cuts between the next two links. Continue on for three or four links. The half links at each end are simply carved off the block. The first full-length link becomes the end of the chain.

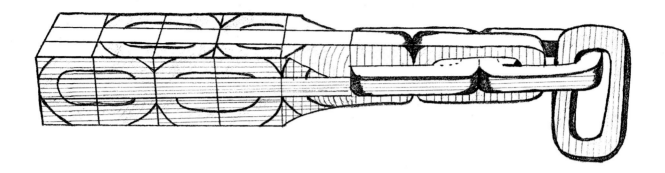

Our next step is to begin to remove a little of the interior of each link. Make stop cuts inside each link. Widen these stop cuts by angling the blade to both sides of your first cut. If you are lining up these cuts on both sides correctly, the knife will cut through. From here on, the block becomes much more delicate. Make light cuts with a sharp blade to ensure both chain and fingers remain unscathed.

Once you have carved through the inside of a link you will be able to complete the separation between two links that we started earlier. Continue making tiny stop cuts from either side until you have cut through.

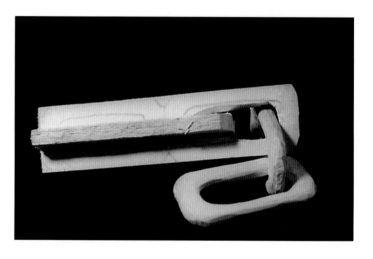

to get a fat curved blade in this tiny space. Take tiny cuts from all angles until you break through. Don't make any attempt to shape or clean up the links until they have broken free from one another. Try to cut a few links free before moving on to new ones.

Clean up the ends of each link. Keep an eye out for the grain direction as you cut. The wood is very weak at these points and requires extremely delicate cuts. Clean up the ends of the links before going on to the sides. Because the sides are lined up with the grain, they are much easier to round off.

You can continue carving the rest of the chain until the block is completely transformed. I like to leave one or two links on my block untouched to show folks a before and after view of the piece.

Chains are also likely to be handled, so apply a basic finish that will seal out dust and fingerprints. Once you've perfected your ball-in-the-cage and your wooden chain, give yourself a promotion to the next level of whittlerdom. Consider treating yourself to a new knife, or at least a new thumb guard.

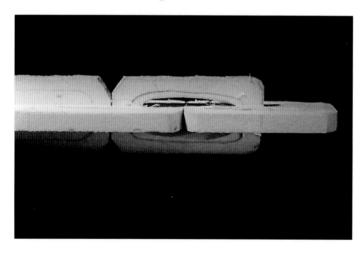

Notice that your links are still joined at their ends. To be sure that you know what wood goes with which link, take a pencil and draw as much of each link on the block as you can. We need to cut through these ends without damaging the links. To accomplish this mean feat, make sure you have a sharp, pointed blade. There just isn't enough room

Four More Whittler's Tricks

Now that we've completed a couple of basic whittling tricks, we can make small design changes to create these new items of interest:

- Arrow Through the Heart
- Ball-in-a-Ball
- Love Spoons on a Chain
- Sliding Hoops

Arrow Through the Heart

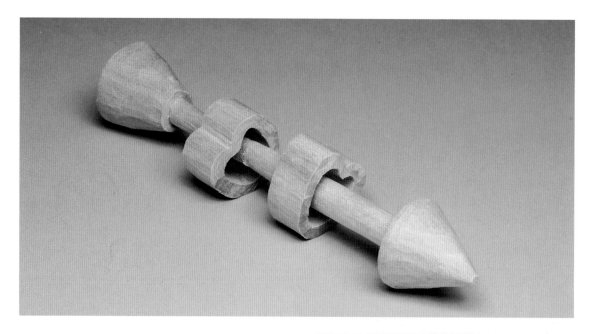

The arrow through the heart is a simplification of the chain—a one-link chain, if you will. Start with a 1" (25mm)-square block about 5" to 6" (127 to 152mm) long. Mark around the block about 1" (25mm) in from each end for the arrow's tip and feather. Pencil in a couple of areas ½" (13mm) in width somewhere in between the tip and feather for hearts. We only require one heart for this project, but you can make multiples and keep the best of the bunch.

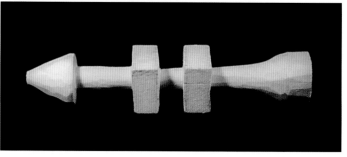

Make stop cuts around both sides of the heart. When you reach the depth of the shaft of the arrow, begin taking tiny cuts on the inside of the heart to release it from the shaft. Don't shape the heart until it is cut free.

Use care in handling the heart, and a sharp blade and delicate cuts to shape it. The entire heart contains short grain and is very weak. You may spend as much time shaping the hearts as you did on the rest of this creation.

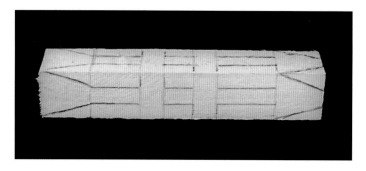

The tip and feather can both be rounded. The point should be carved so it is cone-shaped. Make the shaft about ½" (13mm) in diameter to start out, and then shave it down to ⅜" (10mm) as the carving progresses. The feather is also cone-shaped, with the cone growing out of the shaft.

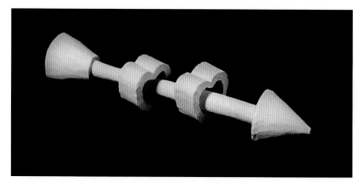

Ball-in-a-Ball

You don't see too many ball-in-a-ball pieces around these days, so you can expect to turn a few heads with this item. It really isn't that much more difficult than the ball-in-the-cage—you just have a round cage.

You first need to carve a ball. Use a sharp blade and the same technique that we learned while carving our egg.

Draw three circles at right angles around the ball (that's one equatorial and two hemispherical for you cartographers). Redraw each line so you have created bands ⅜" (10mm) in width. These bands will be the bars of your cage.

Here are a few things to keep in mind before you begin. The windows to this cage are eight triangular-shaped sections. We'll remove a little out of each window, and then work on freeing the inner ball. Because our windows are so small in relation to the inner ball, we don't have to be as concerned with keeping the ball as large as possible as we did with the ball-in-the-cage. Also, the width of the bars has a direct bearing on their strength, as you might imagine. But keep in mind that the thinner you keep the bars, the easier it will be to free, and then round, the inner ball. I've found that bars ⅜" (10mm) wide and ¼" (6mm) thick work fine on a 2" (51mm)-diameter ball.

Make shallow stop cuts on the lines, and slice away the wood in each window to the same depth. When you reach the desired thickness of the bar, use the very tip of your blade to undercut the bar from each side until it is separated from the ball. Continue cutting and undercutting until the inner ball is completely free. (This will be an event in itself—trust me.)

Shape the ball to a perfect sphere through the windows. When you are satisfied with the inner ball, clean up the bars and the rest of the outer ball.

Love Spoons on a Chain

Once you get the hang of whittling a chain, the next step is to carve objects at the ends of a chain. There are two methods to accomplish this. The time-tested method is to design objects into the end of the block from which your chain is carved so that the object is an integral part of the carving. The shortcut method, also known as the cheater's or "only-God-and-I-will-ever-know" method, is to attach a carving to a pre-carved chain.

I know you won't ever use the cheater's method, but someone might ask you someday how it's done and you should be able to say you've heard that it's done in back alleys under extremely unsanitary conditions by unsavory and unlicensed whittlers for monetary gain. Following the cheater's method, an object is carved with some type of loop incorporated into its design. The end link of a chain is carefully split with the grain, pried open, and this loop is forced (against its will) onto the link. The link is then glued back together, and the whole thing is tagged and hung in some cheap souvenir shop. You'd think there would be laws against this type of thing.

The other end of the spectrum (the time-tested method) involves carving the chain and its accompaniments from a single block. The example I'll use is love spoons connected by a chain. The love spoon is a time-honored object of devotion created by pure-hearted whittlers who want to express their love, as well as by empty-pocketed whittlers with no wheels who just want to impress the babes.

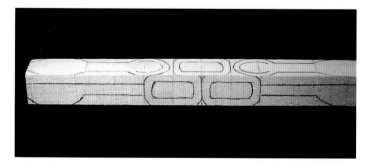

Start with a 1" (25mm)-square block about 12" (305mm) long. Draw a spoon on each end, along with the first link of the chain at the end of each spoon. Add a link to each end until they meet. Alter the size of the center link to hook both sides of the chain together. The spoon shape may be cut with a coping saw or band saw, but the chain will have to be cut out by hand this time. The weave in the spoon handle should be drawn on both sides of the block and traced with shallow stop cuts.

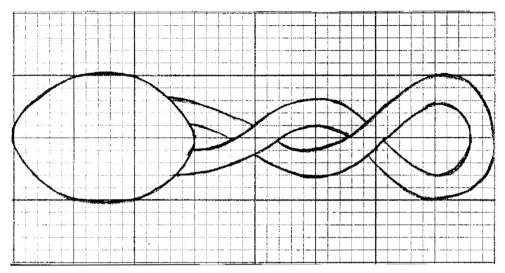

Example spoon design

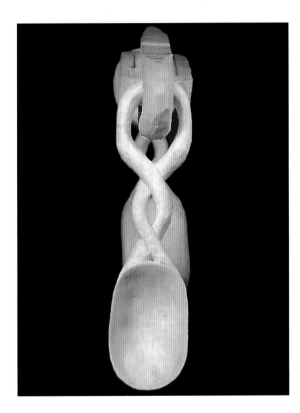

You can drill out the openings to help speed things along, but be sure to make the stop cuts first. They will help to prevent splintering as the bit exits the wood. Using your knife tip, clean out the openings in the weave, the begin rounding the individual cords.

Cutting the concave bowls of the spoons requires a tool such as a gouge or a crooked knife. The design of your tool will dictate how deep you can carve the bowls. Start your cuts at the rim of the bowl and push the wood to the center. Take light cuts both with and across the grain to hollow out the bowl. In the interest of safety, I'm going say this again: take light cuts.

If you have to do any real pushing to get your knife or gouge to cut, you have one of two problems: the blade isn't sharp enough or the cut is too deep. I can tell you some horror stories about gouges slipping from the work and putting stop cuts in various body parts (I have firsthand knowledge of this, if you'll pardon the painful pun). If you don't feel confident making this cut, don't attempt it. Consider clamping the spoon to a bench while you perform this step.

Some tool suppliers even sell a Kevlar glove to protect the hand while making these cuts.

If you don't have the tools to create a concave bowl, try using a succession of sandpaper grits to create a slight hollow in the bowl.

The back of the spoon bowl can be rounded over. If you've gouged out the bowl, whittle the back until the thickness of the bowl wall is about ⅛" (3mm).

Perform the same steps on the other spoon. Don't do your final cleanup on the spoons until the chain is complete. We'll do one final cleanup at that point.

Proceed with the chain carving as described previously.

When the chain is complete, spend time going over the entire piece, as it is sure to be examined by its owner. Use a sharp blade and clean up the edges. Hold the piece at arm's length to examine each link in the chain and every twist in the spoons. Take delicate cuts.

Sliding Hoops

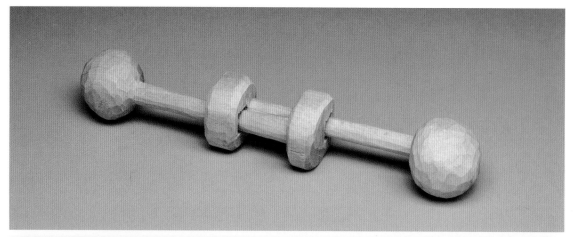

The sliding hoops carving is an odd piece, but it is an attention-grabber and adds to your repertoire of whittling tricks. It looks like a baby's rattle, but its short-grain layout makes it too delicate to stand up to any postnatal gnawing.

Start with a 1" (25mm)-square block about 6" (152mm) long. Whittle 1" (25mm) knobs on each end.

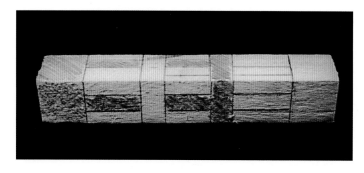

Draw the rest of the parts on the block. The stems are ¼"(6mm) in diameter. Space the hoops 1" (25mm) apart to give yourself clearance to free the stems from the hoops. The stems pass each other in the center, so be sure to leave room for both. The hoops will be positioned off-center in the block. They are only ¼" to ⅜" (6 to 10mm) thick, but make them a little bigger until they've been freed from the stems. Because of the short grain, the hoops won't stand up to rough handling. Take extra care to cut with the grain when shaping the hoops.

Shave down the single stems to a diameter of ½" (13mm). The stems will pass through the first hoop on each side, so make a stop cut at those points. Begin making stop cuts into the side of the hoops.

Pare down the area between the two hoops. Stop occasionally to study this center section to be sure you know which stem is going to connect to which hoop. A stem that passes through both hoops will take away considerably from the trick. As you get the stems lined up, make a stop cut to separate them. Don't be too concerned with cleaning up your cuts until the pieces have been cut free.

Do your final rounding and cleanup on the carving. Make sure that the pieces slide freely through both hoops. Because the strength of wood runs with the grain, opt to skinny up the stems rather than open the hoops too far to remedy a stuck carving.

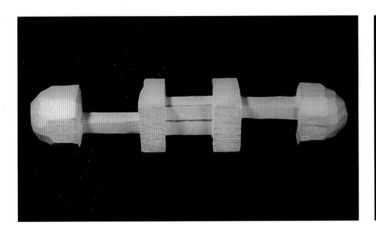

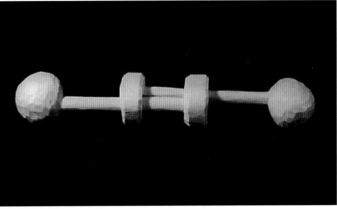

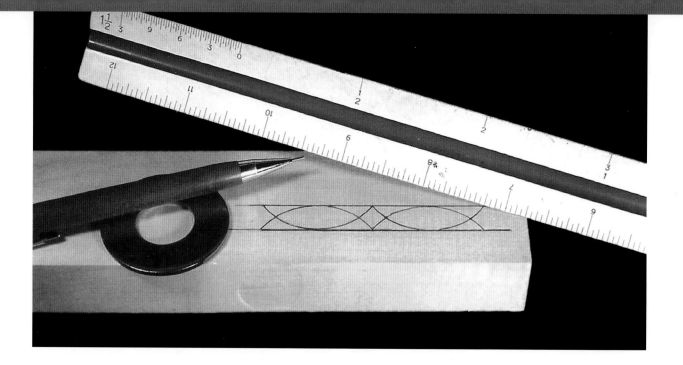

Carving in Shallow Relief

· ·

Up to now, we've been whittling in a mode called in-the-round, or three-dimensional carving. We've had to address all sides of each block because the pieces are meant to be picked up and handled by the viewer. In relief carving, we only concern ourselves with the face of the block. Designs are carved in two dimensions, allowing the shadows created by the cuts to show depth.

Many people gravitate to carving from other woodworking disciplines, such as carpentry or cabinet making. Relief carving is a great way to use your new carving skills to decorate your other woodworking projects. Be sure to practice the design on a scrap piece of wood before cutting up your latest masterpiece.

Our first project will be a border made up of repeating half-circles. When drawing the layout for this project, be sure to use a sharp pencil, or even a mechanical pencil. We'll be following the lines with the tip of our blade, and will be hard-pressed to carve a straight one if our marks are made with a crayon.

Other materials required for this project include a ruler and a template for a 1½" (38mm) circle. I use a ⅝" (16mm) washer that happens to have an outside diameter of 1½"(38mm). Anything close to this size will do. Use any ¾" (19mm) or thicker piece of wood with a clean, flat surface.

Draw two parallel lines ⅜" (10mm) apart. Starting at the end, draw half circles down the board between the parallel lines. Start at the end again and draw another set of half circles in a mirrored image overlapping the first set. Trace one set of half circles with the tip of your blade to a depth of ⅛" (3mm).

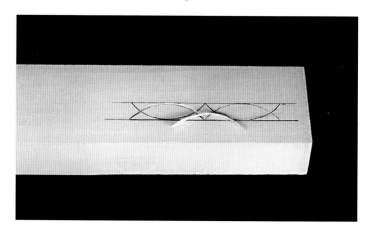

Try to stand your blade up in the wood and use only the tip when cutting. The less metal in the wood, the easier it will be to pull the knife.

Use your thumb as a fulcrum. A rubber thimble from an office supply store on your thumb will keep it from sliding on the work. Let your hand, wrist, and forearm make the cut. If you notice that you are using your upper arm and shoulder for these short cuts, hide the women and children!

You're a loaded gun waiting to go off! One slip and you'll be performing a Zorro imitation on your work, trousers, and opposing thumb. Make sure that your blade is sharp, a minimum amount of metal is in the wood, and you aren't trying to carve hard maple for your first project.

Once the first stop cuts are made, turn the board around and widen the first cuts by angling the blade slightly to the inside of the circle. Tiny ribbons (¹⁄₁₆" [2mm] wide) of wood will peel away as you make these cuts. The object is to keep those ribbons at a consistent width—your work will look much cleaner this way.

Trace the second set of half-circles. Turn the board around and widen these cuts. Notice that the wood is fragile at the point where the lines cross. Be careful with your cuts in these spots.

Grab your ruler and pencil and draw a couple of lines ⅛" (3mm) to the outside of your first two lines for a border. Make a straight-in stop cut on each of these lines. Do these cuts freehand. It helps to look at the line slightly ahead of your blade. Turn your board around and widen each cut by angling your blade slightly to the outside of the rest of the work. Concentrate on keeping the ribbons you slice away at a consistent width.

This little pattern we created can be used as a border for a tabletop, a table skirt, or the face frame on a cabinet. The only requirement for carving a pattern like this is that it needs to be carved into the face grain, as opposed to the end grain, of a board. Practice these cuts before taking on the expensive lumber. Another trial you'll want to make is to cut on the type of wood you are using in your project. If you keep the cuts shallow and just use the tip of the knife, you should be able to carve any of the carving woods I mentioned earlier. Walnut, cherry, and mahogany should be okay, but oak and maple might bring you to your knees.

A variation on our pattern that makes it a little more useful to us as a decoration is to bend it to a curve. Use a compass or template to draw the two parallel lines in an arc ⅜" (10mm) apart. Find and mark the center. Draw the half circles on the inside of the arc first, starting at the center of the arc. Because the length of the outside line is longer than the inside line, the second set of half-circles will need to be lined up with their mirror images one at a time to keep the design balanced.

Cutting the half circles is done in the same manner as described earlier. A border is drawn with a compass or template ⅛" (3mm) to the outside of the first two lines and cut as before.

A curved pattern can be used as a border on curved furniture parts or as a design in itself.

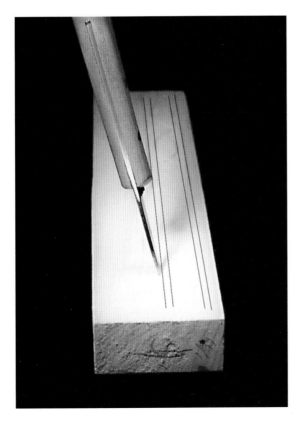

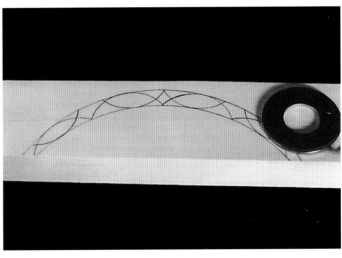

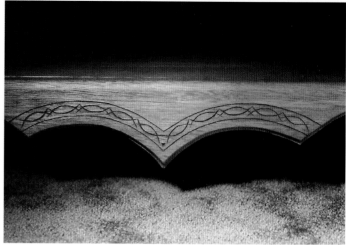

Practice making these triangles at this angle until you can pop them out with just three cuts. The objective is to leave clean cuts and to carve each of the three sides of equal length. The chip-carved triangles are combined with the relief lines to create designs or grouped in geometric patterns as designs of their own.

We've barely scratched the surface, as it were, on chip carving. There are a couple of great books on the subject, as well as a handful of books that contain nothing but designs for chip carving. If you enjoyed this type of carving, I encourage you to check out these other authors and their books.

Carving a simple relief line is a skill that can be used to decorate a number of wooden items. Graceful curved lines can accent any flat surface. Experiment drawing lines freehand on a scrap piece of wood, and then carve the lines.

A small addition we can make to the carved line is the chip-carved triangle. We are going to pop a tiny pyramid of wood out of a board by pushing the tip of our blade in from three different directions so that the tip of the blade ends up at the same point each time. The trick to these cuts is to hold the knife at a consistent angle as you push the blade into the wood.

To make a chip-carved triangle, hold your blade so it points straight down on the wood (a 90° angle). A 45° angle is easy to find because it's half of the 90° angle. Study this angle. The angle we want for chip carving is halfway between 45° and 90°, or about 67°.

The Face

• •

Many carvers consider face carving one of the most difficult areas of woodcarving. This is very true if your intention is to create a representation of a specific person. Caricature faces, however, are another matter entirely. How can you mess up a face that is supposed to be wildly exaggerated in the first place? The worst that can happen is that you end up with an ugly face!

I'm going to describe the steps for whittling a face on the end of a stick. Start with a piece about 1" (25mm) square and at least 2" (51mm) long. Round the top of the block so it appears that a ball is sticking out of the top of the block. Use a slicing cut that starts about ¾" (19mm) down the block and continues out the top. Keep turning the block to a different edge as you carve.

Next we'll define the bottom of the head. Make a mark on an edge 1½" (38mm) below the top of the block to represent the chin. Turn the block 180° and make a second mark 1" (25mm) from the top for the back of the neck. Connect these two marks together with a gentle, sloping line. Make a stop cut on this line, followed by a slicing cut from below to pop out the chip.

Continue turning the block and popping out the chips until you've reached a depth of about ¼" (6mm) all around the block.

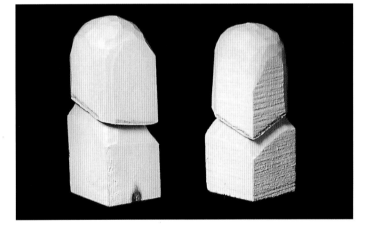

Make a mark on the front edge of the face, halfway from top to bottom. This will be the bottom of the nose. Place your blade just above your mark and make a slicing cut right out from the top of the head. This cut gives the nose the proper profile. Once the profile is established, gently round the edges off the sides and back of your block.

Now let's block in the nose. Draw a very wide V about ¼" (6mm) in width at your mark. Make a couple of stop cuts on the V and slice the wood away from below. Take care as your blade nears the stop cut. We don't want to be knocking the nose off just yet. Keep cutting until the nose sticks out about ¼" (6mm). I like big honkers. There's just more to work with.

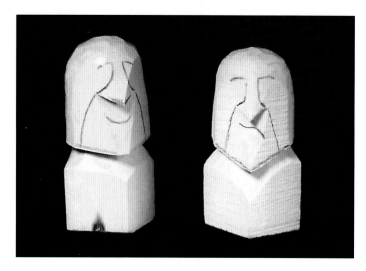

We'll take a quick break from the face to get the hair started. Draw a tiny upside down V on each side of the head at the neckline. Pop out that V with the tip of your blade. Draw the hairline starting at the apex of the V, meeting somewhere on top.

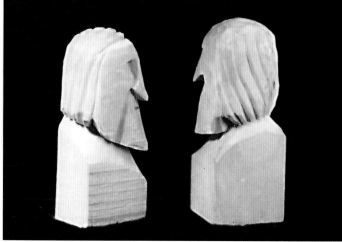

Draw lines to represent the nose, brow line, cheek/jaw line, and the mouth. Better yet, work out the shapes on a piece of paper first, and transfer your favorites to the block.

Start by making the stop cut on the nose lines from the base of the nose to the brow lines. Be sure to hold the knife perpendicular to the block as you cut. Cut the brow line, and then slice away the wood along the nose to a depth of ⅛"(3mm).

Start the slicing cut at the base of the nose and continue it right up to form an eye channel. Use just the tip of your blade to shape the nose. Round over the edges, but take tiny cuts—big ones will make your nose disappear.

Start the jaw/cheek lines just slightly above the base of the nose and take it right out to the neck. Slice away the wood on the mouth side of the stop cuts, and carefully round over the cheeks.

The curve of your line over the top of the head determines the extent of any receding hairline. Use this line as the starting point for the hair. Don't try to carve in individual hairs. Carve a handful of lines as we did with the shallow relief to give the hair direction and texture. Gently carve away what remains of your pencil lines.

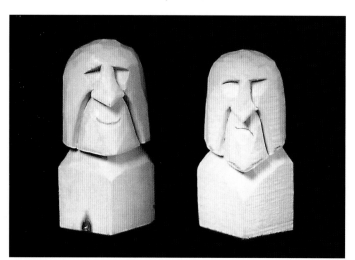

Round off the mouth area and redraw the mouth on our block. Carve the mouth line with a stop cut, and then widen it by angling the blade slightly toward the nose.

To create a lower lip on our face, place the blade 1/16" (2mm) below the mouth and make a quick in-and-down cut toward the chin. We want to scoop a tiny slice from below the mouth, leaving a lip. Round the chin and jaw into the neck.

Eyes, as you might imagine, are the toughest aspect of carving a face. Be sure your knife is extra sharp for this part. Draw a pair of ovals in each eye channel. A rule of thumb is to place the eyes one eye-width apart from each other. The nose you carved may be too wide to fit them in using this rule, however. If so, simply spread them out a little more if you need to.

Pop out triangular chips from the corners of each eye to give them depth. Outline the tops and bottoms of the eyes with stop cuts, and make tiny slicing cuts on the inside of the eyes to help give them a round shape.

For the pupil, we are going to simply make a hole in each eye. Use something that will leave a small, round hole, such as an awl, sewing needle, or thumbtack. Don't use a nail—you'll end up with a four-sided pupil. Press in lightly so you don't split the wood. Also, straight-ahead stares seldom look interesting. Have your character look off to one side or the other.

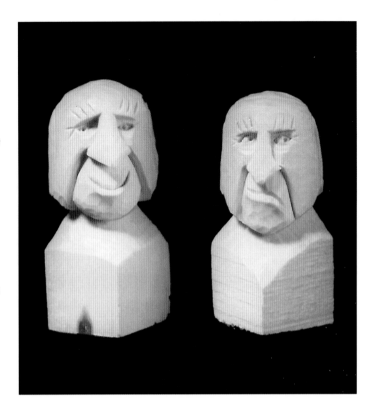

Make curved stop cuts under the eyes to suggest bags, and age them by carving stop cuts out to the sides. That should just about do it for the eyes. Carving and radial keratotomy in one easy lesson!

Place a couple of stop cuts above the brow line for eyebrows. As with the head, don't try to carve individual hairs. Add just a couple on each side to suggest general direction. You can add tiny worry lines across the forehead as well.

More Great Books from Fox Chapel Publishing

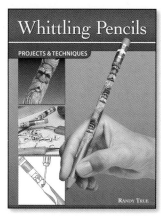

Whittling Pencils
ISBN 978-1-56523-751-3 **$12.99**

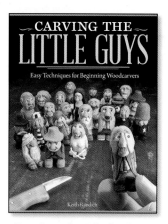

Carving the Little Guys
ISBN 978-1-56523-775-9 **$9.99**

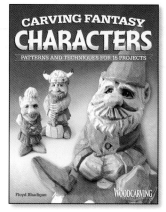

Carving Fantasy Characters
ISBN 978-1-56523-749-0 **$16.99**

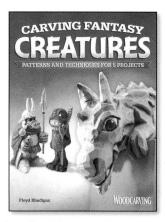

Carving Fantasy Creatures
ISBN 978-1-56523-609-7 **$12.99**

Big Book of Whittle Fun
ISBN 978-1-56523-520-5 **$12.95**

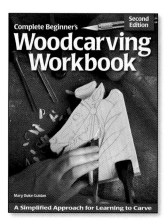

Complete Beginner's Woodcarving Workbook
ISBN 978-1-56523-745-2 **$12.99**

WOODCARVING
ILLUSTRATED

In addition to being a leading source of woodworking books and DVDs, Fox Chapel also publishes *Woodcarving Illustrated*. Released quarterly, it delivers premium projects, expert tips and techniques from today's finest carvers, and in-depth information about the latest tools, equipment, and materials.

Subscribe Today!
Woodcarving Illustrated: 888-506-6630
www.FoxChapelPublishing.com

Look for These Books at Your Local Bookstore or Specialty Retailer or at *www.FoxChapelPublishing.com*